LIFE ON MAYFLOWER

BY JESSICA GUNDERSON

ILLUSTRATED BY BRIAN CALEB DUMM

PICTURE WINDOW BOOKS
a capstone imprint

On a windy September day in 1620, a ship called the *Mayflower* set sail from the coast of England. On board, families huddled together. Children peered around their parents for a last look at the land they were leaving behind. Then, excitedly, they turned their faces to the sea. Ahead was a new life and a new land—America.

The *Mayflower* usually carried goods such as wine and cloth. But on this journey, passengers were her cargo. The *Mayflower* carried 102 passengers and about 25 crew members. It also held two dogs, some goats, chickens, and other animals.

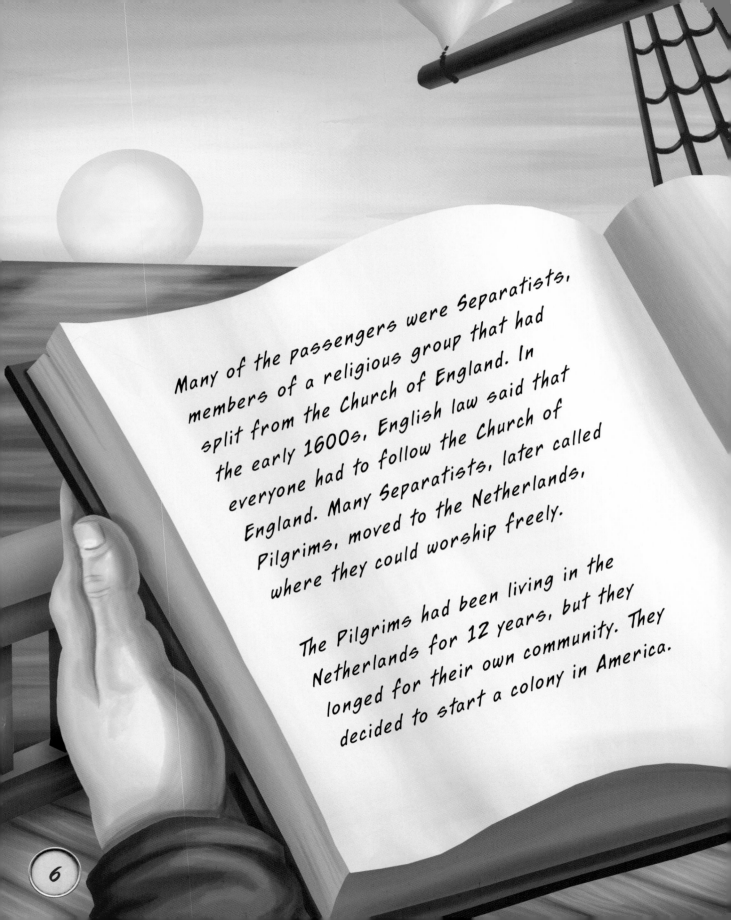

Many of the passengers were Separatists, members of a religious group that had split from the Church of England. In the early 1600s, English law said that everyone had to follow the Church of England. Many Separatists, later called Pilgrims, moved to the Netherlands, where they could worship freely.

The Pilgrims had been living in the Netherlands for 12 years, but they longed for their own community. They decided to start a colony in America.

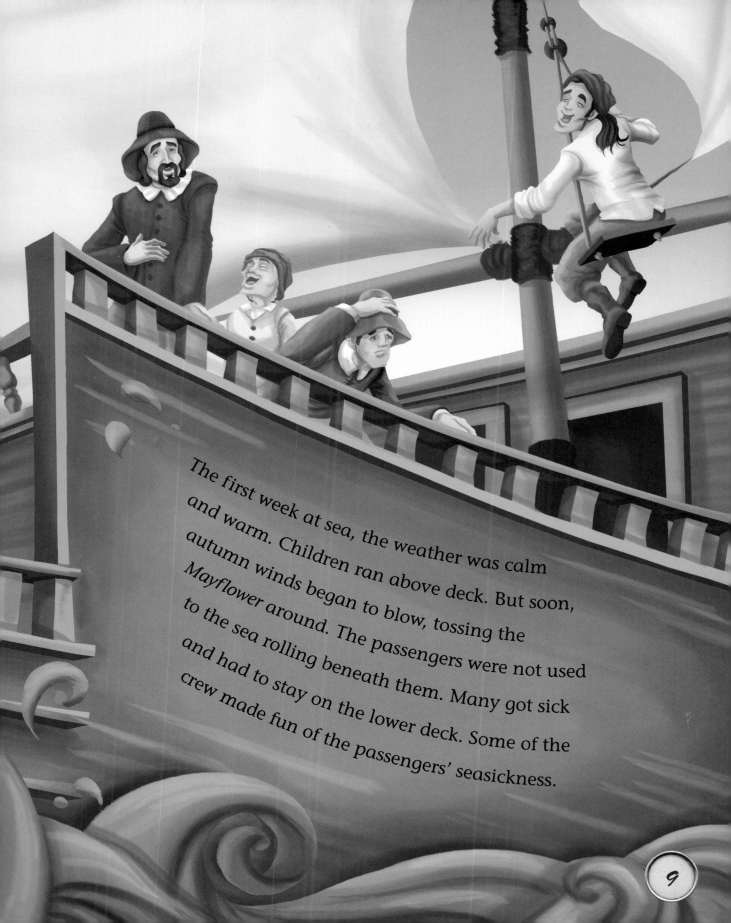

The first week at sea, the weather was calm and warm. Children ran above deck. But soon, autumn winds began to blow, tossing the Mayflower around. The passengers were not used to the sea rolling beneath them. Many got sick and had to stay on the lower deck. Some of the crew made fun of the passengers' seasickness.

The lower deck became the passengers' home away from home. Animals rode there too. It was dark and damp. The ceiling was so low that many adults could not stand up straight. There were no windows. Lanterns supplied the only light.

In the cramped space, children had no room to run. To pass the time, they probably sang or read the Bible. They may have played board games such as Nine Men's Morris, which is like checkers.

With no way to keep food cold on the ship, passengers had to bring food that wouldn't spoil. They ate salted meat, dried peas, hard biscuits, cheese, and oatmeal. With few places on board to cook, passengers made large kettles of stew for everyone to share.

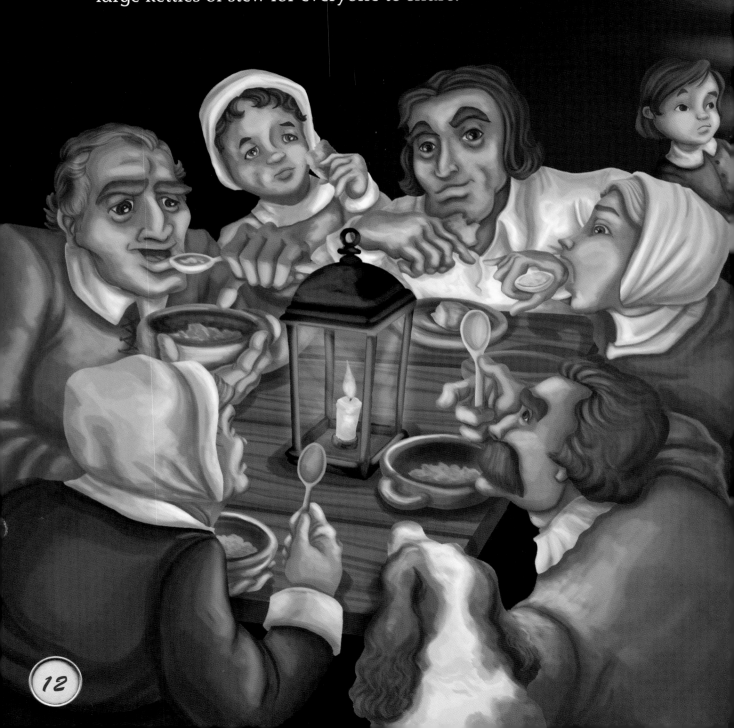

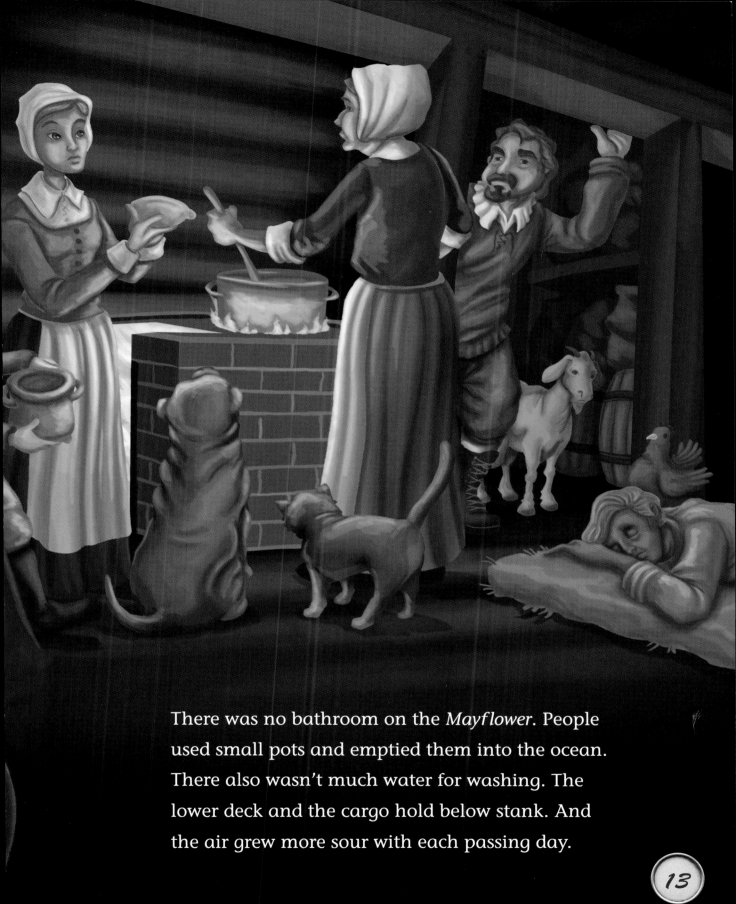

There was no bathroom on the *Mayflower*. People used small pots and emptied them into the ocean. There also wasn't much water for washing. The lower deck and the cargo hold below stank. And the air grew more sour with each passing day.

Out in the Atlantic Ocean, storms could be so strong and loud it seemed like the ship would break apart. One night, terrible winds cracked a wooden beam that supported the ship's frame. Without it, the ship could not sail. Everyone worried the ship would have to return to England. Even some crew members thought the *Mayflower* was doomed.

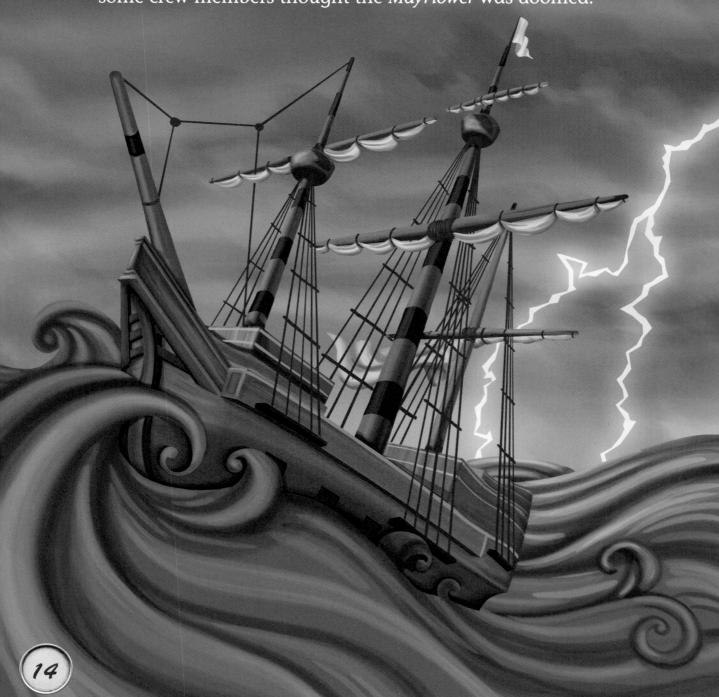

Luckily, one of the passengers had a large iron screw to
hold the beam in place. Once fixed, the ship sailed on.

Another storm threatened the life of a passenger named John Howland. John was above deck when the storm broke. Without warning, strong winds and rain swept him into the ocean. He called for help. No one on board knew what to do.

Then, when all hope seemed lost, John grabbed one of the ship's ropes. Several crew members pulled him back onto the ship. He was wet and cold, but he was safe.

On November 9, after 65 days at sea, the *Mayflower* crew spotted land. But the journey wasn't over yet. The *Mayflower* anchored in Cape Cod while a small group explored the coast.

Native Americans called the Wampanoag were already living there. Unsure of one another, the Wampanoag and the Pilgrims kept their distance.

The Pilgrims learned of an empty village nearby called
Patuxet. There they started building their houses. They
worked on them by day and slept on the ship at night.
The Pilgrims renamed the village Plymouth.

Finally, after almost three months, there were enough homes for everyone. On April 5, the *Mayflower* set sail for England. And a new life began in America for her former passengers.

Timeline of Key Dates

June 1619
The Pilgrims gain permission from the Virginia Company to set up a colony.

September 6, 1620
The *Mayflower* sets sail from Plymouth, England.

November 9, 1620
Land is sighted.

November 11, 1620
The *Mayflower* anchors in Cape Cod. The men sign the Mayflower Compact, an agreement between the passengers to set up a new community.

December 20, 1620
The Pilgrims settle in Patuxet and rename it Plymouth. The Wampanoag had lived there until a few years before, when sickness destroyed most of the village.

December 23, 1620
The Pilgrims begin building.

March 16, 1621
An Abenaki Native American from Maine named Samoset walks into the village. He welcomes the settlers in English. He had learned to speak it from traders he'd met.

March 22, 1621
The Pilgrims sign a peace treaty with Massasoit, a leader of the Wampanoag people. The Wampanoag had lived in the area for thousands of years.

April 5, 1621
The *Mayflower* returns to England with the crew.

Strange But True

On the *Mayflower*, everyone drank beer, even the children. Water was not considered safe to drink.

One baby was born on the journey. The baby was named Oceanus.

Not all *Mayflower* passengers were Separatists. Some were moving to America to better their lives, not for religious freedom. They were later known as "Strangers."

The English the *Mayflower* passengers spoke was a bit different than today's English. Instead of saying, "How are you?" a passenger may have said, "Good day" or "What cheer?" Instead of saying, "Goodbye," he or she may have said, "Fare thee well."

Glossary

anchor—to hold in place with something heavy

cargo—goods carried by ship, airplane, or truck

colony—a place settled by people from another country that follows that country's laws

Pilgrim—one of the people who came to America in 1620 for religious freedom and set up Plymouth Colony; a pilgrim is also someone who goes on a religious journey

Separatist—a member of a religious group that split from the Church of England in the 1600s

spoil—to rot

worship—to pray

Read More

Lassieur, Allison. *The Voyage of the Mayflower.* Graphic Library: Graphic History. Mankato, Minn.: Capstone Press, 2006.

Philbrick, Nathaniel. *The Mayflower and the Pilgrims' New World.* New York: G.P. Putnam's Sons, 2008.

Plimoth Plantation, with Peter Arenstam, John Kemp, and Catherine O'Neill Grace. *Mayflower 1620: A New Look at a Pilgrim Voyage.* Washington, D.C.: National Geographic, 2003.

Internet Sites

FactHound offers a safe, fun way to find Internet sites related to this book. All of the sites on FactHound have been researched by our staff.

Here's all you do:

Visit www.facthound.com

Type in this code: 9781404862845

Check out projects, games and lots more at www.capstonekids.com

Super-cool stuff!

Look for all the books in the Thanksgiving series:

Life on the Mayflower

The Pilgrims' First Thanksgiving

Thanksgiving Crafts

Thanksgiving Recipes

Thanksgiving Then and Now

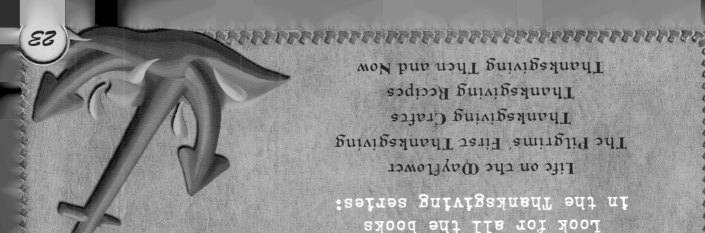

Index

animals, 5, 11
bathing, 13
Cape Cod, 18, 21
children, 2, 9, 11, 22
England, 2, 6, 20, 21
food and drink, 12, 22
games, 11
Howland, John, 16–17
living conditions, 11, 12–13
Massasoit, 21
Mayflower Compact, 21
Patuxet, 19, 21
Pilgrims, 6, 18–19, 21
Plymouth, 19, 21
Samoset, 21
Separatists, 6, 22
setting sail, 2, 20, 21
sickness, 9
Wampanoag, 18, 21
weather, 9, 14, 16

Special thanks to our advisers for their expertise:

Plimoth Plantation
Plymouth, Massachusetts

Terry Flaherty, PhD, Professor of English
Minnesota State University, Mankato

Editor: Jill Kalz
Designer: Alison Thiele
Art Director: Nathan Gassman
Production Specialist: Sarah Bennett
The illustrations in this book were created digitally.

Photo Credits: Shutterstock/Lou Oates, 1, 21, 22,
23, 24 (background texture); Wordpics, throughout.
(typewriter key)

Picture Window Books
1710 Roe Crest Drive
North Mankato, MN 56003
www.capstonepub.com

All books published by Picture Window Books
are manufactured with paper containing at least
10 percent post-consumer waste.

Library of Congress Cataloging-in-Publication Data
Gunderson, Jessica.
Life on the Mayflower / by Jessica Gunderson ; illustrated by
Brian Caleb Dumm.
p. cm. — (Thanksgiving)
Includes index.
ISBN 978-1-4048-6284-5 (library binding)
ISBN 978-1-4048-6719-2 (paperback)
1. Pilgrims (New Plymouth Colony)—Juvenile literature.
2. Mayflower (Ship)—Juvenile literature. 3. Massachusetts—
History—New Plymouth, 1620-1691—Juvenile literature.
I. Title.
F68.G886 2011
974.4'02—dc22
2010033762

Printed in the United States of America in North Mankato,
Minnesota.   032014   008072R